Primitive Poetry

Gerald Braude

Contents

Skies

The High Altitude Sun

One day, I hike up the desolate trail
and rise above the clouds.

My shoulders freeze. My fingers feel blue.
My legs tighten into brittle sticks.
Ice cubes seem to squeeze my toes.

I gasp and gasp for breath.
I reach the mountain peak.
I kick the snow off a log.

One over the other, I place
my mittens on it.
I sit on them and look up.

The sun, a roaring ball of fire,
stares at me, toasts my face,
thaws my bones into heavenly ecstasy.

As the layer of clouds below me
take on the look of snow, the sunrays
split the sky:

Puffs of white smoke below.
A burnt orange inferno above.

A man takes his dog for a walk.
Behind him, his team of bodyguards
perform the scooper duties.

A team of servers place eight menu
entrees in front of him. He samples
each before deciding which one to eat.

At his palatial hangar, he lines up
his corporate pilots and picks the one
who will fly him that day.

Forbes tells me he's up here,
but I don't see him.

Now, only a beautiful blue sky
surrounds the sun. The clouds
are cushy, white pillows.

They tremble, dancing with joy.
Flames flicker up and around them,
embracing and caressing them.

My soul drifts to my head
and whispers, "If this is life
above the clouds, I'll take it."

Operation Mockingbird

The glacier atop the magic mountain
sparkles under the radiant moon.
Professor Schwab's bald head
sparkles, too, as does
his tactical bulletproof vest.
He announces in broken
particles of English,
"Build back better."

The message soars
through the crisp, clean,
mountain air down
to the gathering fog
around the mop
of a British prime minister.
In clearer English, he finishes
his announcement,
"Building back better."

The state-of-the-art global
communications systems
push the message through
the swirling North Atlantic
winds to a prime minister
with a salt and pepper goatee.
In more precise English, he
finishes his announcement,
"Has created an opportunity
to build back better."

As the northerly winds guide
the message down the darkening
fog of the Atlantic Coast,
a white-haired president comes
up with a better variation.
"We can't just build back.
We gotta build back better."

With the winds dying down,
an army of Democratic
congressmen march along the party
line across the length of the country
before deploying their forces
along the smoldering Pacific Coast.

From the thirty-third congressional
district in California
to the second and sixth congressional
districts in Washington,
they simply say,
"Build back better."

When the next radiant moon
illuminates Professor Schwab's
bald head, his message soars
down the magic mountain
in broken particles of English.
"You'll own nothing.
And you'll be happy."

Current Electric

In Green Preserve Canyon,
his running mate at his side,
like a lightning conductor
the white-haired man

thunders,
"After you elect us,
 We will require masks
nationwide."

The crowd roars
in applause.

A glowing red cloud claps
echoes,

"Masks
hide
who
we
are."

High Altitude Observation

After the lockdown lifted slightly,
I rose above the understory.

My foothills were covered
with flat needles of firs.

Covered with hairs of furrowed bark,
my legs ascended along the other tree trunks.

I filled my gut from the streams
rolling into the lake of angels.

With gravel-covered shoulders, I reached
a ridge of high altitude ecstasy.

I slowed my pace to take it all in:
Gods of gleaming white mountains
sparkling blue skies
a pure-colored sun.

The air effortlessly slid through my nostrils.
Pounding footsteps shook my shoulders.

A hiker maneuvered around a set of rocks
and then toward me.

I courteously stepped off the trail.
I almost made out his facial features.

He placed a surgical mask over his nose and mouth,
sidestepping and stumbling to the deep outlines

on the other side of the trail as if my top
were blowing fierce winds and fire.

I scratched my head and looked back.
Sure enough, he was removing his mask.

I lowered my elevation to the firs and stumbled
upon a wind-tattered mileage sign.

Carvings on its back
read, "Free the sheep."

Milky Way

I dream about her.
I wake up to reality.

How do I turn this dream
into a reality?

How do I turn this reality
into a dream?

Mission Planet Earth

I was blindsided
by the hysteria
of the masses hiding
behind their adobe walls.

I was blindsided
by the rituals
of masks
and needles.

I was blindsided
by the transformations of men
into women, women into men,
or somewhere in between.

My log entries always start
with, "What kind of a mess
did I get myself
into."

Shifts

Plate Tectonics

I stand alone
on a mountain peak.

Below me, pillows
of clouds flow by.

A wisp of cirrus
breaks away.

It rises far above
my head.

As it obscures
the sun, I wonder.

Amidst a land below
of war, illness, and famine,
why am I always trying
to outsmart
the prevailing narrative?

Teach Your Children

The shots from downtown
Dallas were heard
around the world.

Fidel Castro tossed away his cigar,
staggered to the Bay of Pigs,
dropped tears into the saltwater.

Nikita Khrushchev tossed away his vodka glass,
pounded his palms against the east side
of the Berlin Wall, and sobbed.

Ho Chi Minh tossed away his copy
of the US Declaration of Independence
and dropped tears into a rice paddy.

In the classrooms surrounding the shooting gallery,
students remained silent, staring quizzically
at one another, save those under their desks.

When the news came
through the loudspeakers,
they jumped to their feet.

Desks, chalkboards, and floors shook
from the echoes
of stomping, dancing, and cheering.

Progress

Every town has a river.
Split River Valley is no different.

The edge of town greets you with a gas
station. Puddles of potholes surround
pumps devoid of digital card slots.

The pump handles are laden with rust.
The store windows are boarded up,
and the front door handle is missing.

First came the electric cars,
then word got out the owner
was putting water into the gasoline.

As a courtesy to its customers,
the plant-based grocery on the other
side provides rows of electric car outlets.

The smoothly paved riverwalk leads you to
the town tavern. Cigarette butts and puddles
of potholes surround the two parked cars.

Behind the dusty window hangs a photo
of Gene Autry and the backs of two men
in big-rimmed hats and plaid, flannel shirts.

One sips a can of Budweiser,
the other a can of Pabst.
The tavern sells no other kind.

On the other side, rows of
glistening grapevines surround
the tasting room/store.

Outside and under a tarp, violinists,
cellists, and a drum machine blare
the new Ravel through their amps.

The clientele stand, sit, pat one another
on the back, yell, and yell some more
through life-can't-better-than-this smiles.

Inside the continuously swinging door,
one yells after the other,
"Let me sample that one next."

Behind the bar and ringing register, the owner
smiles to his wife. "Can't think of a better way
to invest my inheritance."

The still smoothly paved riverwalk then leads
you to the corner store. Save the cigarette butts,
the paved lot is empty.

Past the flashing "Open" sign on the door, you
can pay cash for cigarettes, cheap booze
and chemically processed Hostess goodies.

On the other side, car drivers fight for parking
spaces so they can shop at the bowling alley
turned into organic food co-op.

And they're willing to tap top dollar
for these live longer-and-better microbrews,
local wines, and natural energy bars.

The riverwalk continues without a crack
to the town's tourism hub:
The Split River Wharf.

A building called The Victorian is the centerpiece.
Hand-in-hand, a couple flick on the Grand Opening
sign for their retirement dream olive oil store.

But their first customers plug their noses before sampling
the vast assortments of finely-picked products.
Down the hall is that beer-battered fish and chips joint.

After the sun sinks below the riverside, a chubby man,
his apron laden with grease, frowns and puts up
a Closed for Good sign on the window.

It is next to a sign posted by the landlord:
Lawsuit Filed for Violation of Lease Agreement.

Change

On my twenty-first birthday,
my wife hopped into our trailer
and handed me a package
from her parents.

I pulled out a T-shirt.
Between "God Bless"
and "America" was
a USA flag.

We looked at each other and giggled.
I dumped it into the waste basket
below me.
We roared in laughter.

A quarter century later,
when the Chinese Communist Party
virus hit the news,
this was no longer a laughing matter.

From the far end
of our neighborhood,
my in-laws called me
at our house:

Health officials clad
in white with red trim,
holding syringes,
were marching from door to door.

I burst out the door.
Without saying a word,
I rushed past my wife and kids
on the front lawn.

I sprinted past the community
church, barn, clinic, grange,
and school, and rushed
into Sam's General Store.

A ran up and down rows
of merchandise adorned
with Made in America labels
until I found it:

A white baseball cap
embroidered with a USA flag
brandishing our forefathers'
circle of thirteen stars.

I held it to my heart
pumping me
with live free
or die pride.

I dropped two
twenties on the front
counter and told the young
lady to keep the change.

Depends

It's best to start
a memoir, novel,
short story, or poem
with an attention grabbing
hook. Here's an example:

I used the word nigger.

Dusk

On our wedding day,
my wife's eyes
sparkled
like the ring
I put on her finger.

Two decades to the day
later, I look into her eyes.
I find myself searching,
searching to see whether she
has been drinking.

The New Normal

I sit on gravel beside
my wife's gravesite.
I am no longer in a position
to criticize other parents.

Yes, our son won the scholarship,
awarded top of his class,
hit the big-time salary.
But where did I go wrong?

For the greater good, he took
DNA altering shots. He changed
his name. Before he moved
out, I folded his dresses and bras.

He got *Blazing Saddles* banned
from the library because it used
the N-word. I drop a tear
on her site.

The water sizzles and says,
"What are you talking about?
This is the twenty-first century,
you dummy. He's doing great!"

Old Man's Blues

How can I
keep my son's
happiness from making
me unhappy?

How can I
keep my son's
misery from making
me miserable?

Duelers

Survival of the Fittest

Better to die in battle for my faith
than rot in old age from disease.

On the other side of the line:
Yes sir, I'm here to die for my country.

In a dusty, 1914 Jerusalem train yard, fighting age
Frenchmen and Germans answer their mobilization
calls for Europe, shouting their national songs
from their respective cars.

Time for the climactic college gridiron classic.
Lights, camera, action.

The ABC announcer:
These two teams do not like each other.

The ESPN announcer across the state line:
Between these two teams, nothing but bad blood.

Comparisons

Simile:
War is like a drug addiction.

Metaphor:
War is a drug addiction.

Modern Legislation

Another week of pure partisan
voting is done.

Amongst the microphones and cameras,
the senator hovers over the rostrum.

His rapid answers refer to unity
to rescue our fellow Americans.

"Before I go watch the Nationals
play ball, any other questions?"

A hand is raised. A blank reporter's
notebook dangles from the other hand.

"As for your sports reference, I understand
your football team is no longer the Redskins."

"That's right. It reflects who we are
here in Washington: Team.

"In that case, isn't it better
to name them the Robots?"

Arab Bashing

Who would have ever thought
passing a fake bill
would create a public uproar?

But black leaders say
the victims committed a bigger crime:
Calling the tax-funded police.

The victims' punishment:
"Fuck CUP Foods" in drooping
blood-colored paint on their store's exterior.

Beyond this justice
of vengeance, one question
remains:

If owned by blacks,
would the store
have been vandalized?

Clipped Wings

I only fear
a dictator's
paranoia.

Intimidation

He stands with his back to the flaming wood stove.
He wears a smudged gray sweatshirt and faded blue jeans.
Below his charcoal curly hair, his eyes sag.
His deeply dimpled cheeks twitch.

"It's about time you people got here!"
He accusingly waves
the letter of warning at her.

She is framed by a ten-by-ten entrance.
A white dress runs tightly down the
contours of her pin-shaped body.
A breeze brushes past her flaming red hair.

A young couple slither
along a gossamer of sunlight
past her. They tell him
they are hungry.

"Do you have your vaccination cards?"
The couple look down and shake their heads.
"That's okay. You're already in our designated
outdoor dining area."

He leads them to a table beside the wood stove.
He opens the hatch, tosses the letter into the flames,
and pivots. His beer belly bulges just below
her pair of tea cups.

His beer breath barks into her pale face
and flaming red lipstick, "If anyone
is ever going to shut this restaurant down,
it's going to be me, not you!"

Slightly hunched over,
she wanders from one fallen leaf
to another, an inspector looking
for clues, perhaps.

Moments pass. She fixes her gaze
on the halfway opened window.
"This needs to be another half-inch open."
He slides the window.

She cocks her head
and wiggles her nose.
"Another quarter-inch
and we'll leave you alone."

Protecting the Elderly

They sit across from each other.

"It's been a long time, Grandpa."

"Well, I feel better protected now."

"What do you mean?"

"I just got a booster. Speaking of which, why are you not vaccinated?"

"Because I won my court case."

"And you're here, anyway."

"You are my grandpa, aren't you?"

"Where's your mask?"

"Dad calls that child abuse."

"Then you need to move your chair back."

"How's that?"

"A little more."

"How's that?"

"That's fine."

Trenches

Romantic Dining

The lady in a tight, satin shirt
places the burger deluxe plates
on the ammonia aroma table.

Burger juices bleed
into the jumbo fries,
covered with ketchup.

"Be right back
with your double chocolate
syrup shakes," she says.

The couple across from each
other remove the M95s
from their jumbo cheeks.

"The perfect solution to the virus
is simple," one says. "Just eat
during all waking hours."

A fry dangles from the mouth
of the other. "The reason
behind this logic is?"

"Notice that when we masticate,
we're allowed to remove these masks,
but when we're done…"

The barrel-shaped shakes
thud onto the table. "We
have to put them on again."

"Meaning transmissions
don't occur during chewing
and swallowing."

"Yes, we should
graze all day like herds
of sheep."

"Isn't that what we are, anyway?"

Robots

Tomorrow was the big event.
The game plan was set.
All they had to do was carry
out their duties.

On his bed, he caressed
the golf club beside him
and the golf balls
in his pocket.

The snoring began
and pages on the annals
of constitutional democracy
flashed into his head:

"Though their elections were twenty years apart,
though they were from different political parties,
both Gore and Trump conceded their elections
with class and dignity."

He snapped
out of bed,
his fingers trembling
as he clutched his golf club.

He staggered to the lectern.
He yelled to his followers.
His opponent won fair and square.
Let's go home and play golf.

With fixed stares,
The mob swiveled
and headed
to the lowering sun.

Down the avenue,
his followers on the hill
withdrew their objections
to the vote count.

Their capitol was devoid
of broken windows or doors.
Nothing was stolen from
any congressional leader.

A police officer
and four others
lived
to tell about it.

Slavery

Columbus enters the cathedral
and sees the landed owner
and a few Merino sheep
slip out the back door.

The white-haired priest
appears at the pulpit.
"We must follow
the word of God."

In the name of the Holy Trinity,
Columbus hops on his ship
and sails again to the New World
to retrieve more of those naked slaves.

When he reaches the white-foamed shoreline,
his temples twitch, and his eyes moisten.
This is not the New World
but a different world.

He enters the White House press room
and sees the chairman of Pfizer
and a few in lab coats
slip out the back door.

The white-haired president
appears at the rostrum.
"We must follow
the rules of science."

Think Globally, Act Locally

Do your part.
Get the jab.
Think of our kids.

Our parents.
Our elderly.
Our country.

Think of the best part:
You might win
Shirley Jackson's lottery.

Test Tubes

The white-haired president
squirms on his throne.

Piles of religious exemption
petitions crawl up his shins.

He looks down
to his press secretary.

"I just don't
get it."

He looks to the top
of the Capitol Dome.

"Why settle for God
when you can have science?"

Another Record Breaking Quarter for Walmart

Outside the mainstream narrative,
complaints about PCR tests abound.

Its inventor says the tests are not
for diagnosis.

The cycle thresholds are manipulated
toward false positives.

They'll drill a hole through
your pocketbook.

Our Walmart associates
have the perfect solution for all that.

We have COVID-19 tests you can take
in the privacy of your home.

In our spirit of pay less, live more
you get two tests for the price of one.

Best of all, these tests are FDA authorized,
and if you can't trust the FDA, who can you trust?

MK Ultra for the New World Order

A cracked two-lane highway
is flanked by green embankments.

A green rectangular sign with a white profile
of George Washington's bust hangs overhead.
The white lettering reads,
"Freedom Memorial Scenic Route."

Before a driver can finish singing
the "Star Spangled Banner,"
an overhead neon scoreboard comes into view:
weather reports, traffic conditions, ferry alerts.

Before one can finish singing,
"God Bless America," the sign changes:
"We're all in this together.
Stay at home orders in effect."

Before one can finish reciting
the Pledge of Allegiance, the sign changes:
"We're all in this together.
Come out and mask up."

Before one can finish reciting
the Bill of Rights, the sign changes:
"We're all in this together.
Go get vaxed."

For the Greater Good

Mr. Washington lives in the only state
named after a president.
His manifest destiny is to cross
the street and catch the ferry on time.

A baritone sings for spare change,
cars honk, a bus screeches to a halt.
The chiming church bell
is conspicuously missing.

The light turns green,
and the "Walk" sign flashes on.
He rushes off the curb, onto the sidewalk,
into a flashing fender.

The wheels flatten him to the loose
pebbles and striped asphalt.
His eyes point toward the fading
license plate.

Two policemen enter the swirl
of gritty dust. A torn front cover
of the tabloid *The Stranger*
whirls in a spiral past them.

The policeman cuts and rolls
up Mr. Washington's shirtsleeve.
He scans his smartphone
along the writhing arm.

"Tattoo?" the other officer asks.

"Nope. Virus risk."
He stands tall
and juts out his chin.
"Let him rot in hell."

A hanging helicopter fades into the fog.

Pale men break out from cracked
glass doors of swaying skyscrapers,
blinking and maneuvering
around the body.

One points
and laughs.
"Looks like a pancake
with tomato sauce."

The dull air darkens.
The light turns red,
The red "Don't Walk"
sign remains on.

Cross traffic stops for the lady
with red brick arms.
She hums the melody to
"He's Got the Whole World
in His Hands," a singsong
rhythm to the swaying
of her Gates Foundation handbag.

One of her clogs pins
a shirtsleeve to the ground.
She bends sideways
and spits on his arm.

Big Brother Grocery

I have been standing in line
long enough to have eaten
all the rows of candy bars.

Finally, through my mask,
I say to the cashier, "We
miss you in the neighborhood."

A muffled tone reverberates
through his mask. "You got
to move when you got to move."

I slap the sales flyer on the counter
and rub my thumb on the picture
of organic frozen blueberries.

"I need a raincheck
on those pebbles
of antioxidants."

The cashier yanks his smartphone
out of his apron. "A shipment
comes in tomorrow."

"That's exactly
what your boss
told me yesterday."

He pulls a slip of paper out of the drawer.
The line behind me lengthens; some glued
to their smartphones, others to the candy bars.

His pen scribbles the month and date,
then stutters. "I keep wanting to write
1984."

I lean down to the raincheck and laugh
an air of camaraderie. "I'll say hi
to George Orwell for you."

"I hear you."

Dumpster Diving

The climactic moment
from our instructor's
week-long buildup has come:
It's dumpster diving day.

I step into the sun. I pass
an instructor and students
from another workshop
at a picnic table littered

with tattered books,
pens, scraps
of paper,
and shot glasses.

I leap into a rusty dumpster,
and I find myself
in a canyon
of concrete details.

I gather the items of interest.

The kind of leather glove Jackie Kennedy
would wear only it has holes at the fingertips.

A rust-colored broadleaf maple
with scribbles of indiscernible ink.

A pile of ripped sheets of hard, glossy paper.
Immigration papers, perhaps.

A tree branch carved
into the shape of a pointed pencil.

A smoke stained candle
with "I love you" sketched into it.

I leap out of the dumpster,
juggling ideas in my arms.
I approach city hall and recognize
a person from the mugshot

atop of his daily column.
His chest resting on his paunch,
he peers through his
bottleneck glasses and scribbles

into his reporter's notebook.
I raise my chin, trying to sneak a peek.
He smiles at me, revealing
his row of daggers.

"That's right," he says.
"There's no shortage
of shit
to write about."

King of the Hill

I type another perfectly persuasive
sentence. An ant pops from the keyboard
and marches across my touchpad.

I squish it and brush it away.
My document disappears from the screen.
Almost by magic, I make it reappear.

I type another perfectly persuasive
sentence. Seemingly from nowhere,
an ant marches across my touchpad.

I pound the keys as it scurries along
the keyboard walls onto the wide open
screen. I squat it and swat it away.

I type onto the screen: I don't get it.
The house and I are spotless, and I treat
you guys like dirt. But you keep following me.

Like dust particles, ants swarm onto the screen.
The tablet mode icon turns on. The screen reads,
"Because you're a great leader."

Dreams

The Great American Dream

The room is filled
with red, white, and blue.
A liver-spotted hand drops a bulging envelope
on the recruiter's desk:

Three-hundred-dollars just as we did
in the Civil War.
It's for my son's liberty.
I'm his replacement.

It's a win-win for us both.
Badly needed money for your treasury;
I'm assured those Vietnamese
won't blow my son's balls off.

My age?
I'm too old to have any more kids.
So if I get my balls blown
off, what's the big deal?

Bravery?
Did I not paratroop over Normandy?
Did I not sweat out my adult life building
cluster bombs for Honeywell?

They were good to me,
but all that money ain't
gonna get me grandkids if my
son's balls are blown off.

See my logic?

Psychologically unfit?
You mean like sending our
young men to battle to get their balls
blown off?

Tom Joad

Hands in my pockets, I stroll
into my fourth straight ghost town.

I whistle a counter melody
to a song from the wind.

Doors and shutters squeak open
and bang close. I stop.

The high plains drifter breaks
through the flickering fog.

Muscles bulge against flapping
shirt sleeves.

A sharp V-back leads
down to his belt.

A syringe juts from each side holster.
A row of needles line the back of the belt.

He removes four of them. His fists hammer
two of them to a wall.

A break in the fog reveals the top
of a flyer:
Wanted Dead or Alive

He hammers in the bottom two needles.
I squint at the middle line:
For Crimes against Children

The wind picks up, howls,
kicks up the dust.

The high plains drifter shrugs.
Back perfectly straight, he strolls

against the wind and disappears
into a patch of fog.

The wind blows off the top two needles.
The flyer flaps wildly.

Just before it breaks and flies
away, I make out the bottom line:
Big Bird

Public Health in a Dream World

To Lilian Franck

Mr. Gates stands at the podium
and addresses the WHO:

"Our priorities are your priorities."

The director at the long table
violently shakes her head.

"I can't believe I heard what I
just heard. Please repeat that."

Mr. Gates adjusts his glasses. With clarity
and precision, he repeats himself.

The director slams down her fist.
"How can you be so arrogant?"

"We fund only worthy priorities."

"Well, you can take your damn
money and shove it."

"I'll see to it you
pay for that statement."

"Get out of this hall
before I have security remove you."

Walkin' with Miles of Horns

The blues howl
after midnight
through
a cellar door.

Yes, blues howl
through
a shakin' door
into the night.

Yes, I'm walkin'
today.
I'm walkin'
tomorrow.

I'm walkin'
to play.
I'm walkin'
to blow.

I'm walkin'
with my feet.
Happy beat.

Walkin' down
the street.
Yeah!

Intuition

I passed the gate and asked
a greeter, "Where's
the smartest man alive?"

He or she, hard to tell
in the dusk, pointed to the end
of the alley.

I stomped and swayed
against the gusts of wind.

Finally, I found myself
on a chessboard.

I could only make
out the fluorescence in his eyes
and his pointed, white beard.

I asked him, "Are you the one?"
The answer came with a turned up
palm, a shrug, and in a sorry way.

"All we can do in life
is make an educated guess."

A Historical Perspective

I can't believe
I am a hundred
years old.

How this came
to be,
I do not know.

Except to say, we are no
different now than we were
back then.

Vacation Home

I hear it over and over again.

He is going to his vacation rental.
She is going to her vacation rental.

The couple are going to their vacation rental.
The family is going to their vacation rental.

I stand on the roof of my longhouse.
I look out.

To my neighbors tending to their plants or scrap
metal, or chasing their kids down the driveway.

To the hordes of tourists pouring past
the "Victorian Arts Community"
sign even though this is a paper mill town.

To the sun beaming down on the glacier
capped mountains. To the open, alpine ridges.

To the waterfalls flanked by alders, maples,
firs, and cedars. To the rivers and streams spilling
into the ponds, lakes, and straits.

To the islands spread out below the glacier
capped mountains beyond.

I soak it all in. This is my only home,
but it is my vacation home.

* 9 7 8 9 3 9 5 2 2 4 6 5 9 *